# Words on \

*Inspired by*

## David North

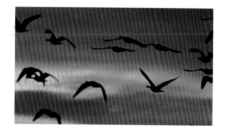

A limited first edition of 3,000 copies

Published in 2006 by Birdseyeview Books/Wild Norfolk
Copyright © 2006 David North

All rights reserved. No part of this publication may be reproduced in any form or by any means,
without permission in writing from the publisher, except for brief passages in a review.

# Wild Wood

Wild wood

where the trees whisper,

remembering.

And you can listen to ancient stories

told in soft leaf songs.

*Sheringham, May*

# Early Spring Hazel Hedge

Catkin waterfalls
Brighten hedgerows.
Yellow cascades
Ripple in the wind
Above the blackthorn foam.

*Itteringham, February*

# Everyday Miracles

Dawn and dusk mysteries,

the ancient ones.

Tides of changing light ebb and flow,

washing the world with colour

as the earth turns.

*Aldborough, September*

# Poppies

Poppy show-offs,
in tissue-thin red party frocks.
Diaphanous dazzlers,
you wear your scarlet dress
                    for a day only,
then cast it off at night
                    with gay abandon.
But what a party trick,
to dance with the wind
and scatter seeds down centuries
from pepper-pot time capsules.

*Cromer, June*

# What is it about gulls and tractors?

What is it about gulls and tractors?

They follow tractors everywhere

shouting their admiration

in raucous crowds.

*Fenland, ploughed fields, October*

# Nothing moves
# on the heath

The still heat of midday.

Nothing moves on the heath

except the adder's tongue.

A landscape dissolves into a shimmering haze

of patchwork colours,

gorse yellow, birch green, heather purple.

Nothing moves on this heath

except me, and the adder's tongue.

*Kelling, August*

# On reflection

On reflection,
Even puddles have
Their hidden depths.

*Holkham after showers, November*

# Crows

Wind-blown crows
scattered across a storm-grey sky.
They dance,
falling like dark leaves
into the gathering darkness.
Calling, cawing, tumbling,
as they fly to roost.

*Thurgarton woods, November*

# Tree Tales

Nature's tall story
                    the tree
You hold the wisdom of centuries
With quiet grace in your branches

*Felbrigg, September*

# Snow Buntings

A flurry of snow buntings,
wind-blown wanderers out of the north,
vanish like melting snowflakes
into the sands.
Then, lifting on the wind,
these dancers in black and white
fly onwards, over dune, marsh and creek
into the grey distance.

*Holkham, January*

# Bee Orchids

Fallen to earth, half-hidden
      amongst green grasses
Cowled bee angels
      with pink wings
Strange beauties,
with deceit in mind.

*Burnham Overy, June*

# Gulls hang on the wind

Gulls hang on the wind
Above waves that surge and roar
Beyond a line of shingle
Vast space
An emptiness
Water sky and silence

*Blakeney Point, May*

# Bluebells

Entering the wood

I stood on the shore of a bluebell lake

unfathomable violet depths

stretching becalmed

under green leaf clouds.

*Blickling, April*

# Hedgerow

How many centuries have you stood
marking the seasons?
White thorn blossom welcoming summer,
red haws bringing in the autumn.
Once you marked the line of an ancient drove
and cattle munched your shoots.
Under your shelter,
fox path, rabbit run, weasel lair.
Pheasants reared their chicks
safe in your thicket.
Hares nursed their leverets,
fawns lay hidden.
Was it centuries ago or yesterday
when birds brought you wildling seeds?
Hazel, blackthorn, cherry, crab,
all found a nursery under your cover.
Holly, oak and ash came too –
forgotten century markers.
In appearance, not a special hedge,
low, gapped and close-ploughed.
But flail this hedge
and you flail history.

*Mannington, May*

# Fulmars

Along red and white cliffs
stiff-winged fulmars patrol.
They hang,
suspended like kites in the wind,
riding the cliff updrafts,
their laughter echoing from
carstone and chalk.

*Hunstanton, April*

# Ivy feast

Have you heard?
It's an ivy berry feast.
Wood pigeons hang like parrots,
Spread-wing gluttons
at the hedgerow banquet.
Blackbirds feast on black berries
stabbing with yellow beak daggers.
Late winter trees bare-branched,
larders empty, autumn fruits long gone.
But here the party's on.
Shiny green leaves edged silver with the night's frost.
No invitations required at this berry free for all
All welcome at nature's take-away.

*Thurgarton, February*

# Pinkfeet

Skeins of geese pattern winter skies
ebbing and flowing like dawn and dusk tides
across boundaries of land, sea and sky.

*Brancaster, December*

# Fleeting glimpses

Fleeting glimpses
                of your hidden lives,
Hare, badger, otter, vole,
Kith and kin, close relatives,
Like us, yet unlike,
Parallel worlds, parallel lives,
Mysterious and secret.

*Houghton, October*

# Pheasant

Dressed to kill, Strutting his stuff.

Car passes, Murder scene (seen).

*Baconsthorpe, March*

# Swifts

Inky black night shadow bird
screaming against blue skies.

Einstein's bird, you know the equations
Energy momentarily materialised as bird,
Time and space meet at the point of your scream
Your black wings cut across days, nights and continents
And your passage marks my summers.

*Holt, June*

# Swallowtails

Swallowtails,
dancers in black and gold,
celebrating summer sun.
Less serious in your flight
　　　　　　　than dragonflies,
playing tag round ragged robin
you are the acrobats of
　　　　　　　sedge and fen.

*Strumpshaw Fen, June*

# Old Hushwing

A white owl flies on white wings

Through a white world

Falling snow, falling silence,

And at the still centre

A white owl flies on white wings.

*Hickling, December*

# Notes

### Page 3 - Photographer: Martin Hayward Smith

Today's woodlands lack many of the large mammals which originally played vital roles in their ecology. Wildwoods were once home to beavers, bears, wild boar and wolves. Do the trees remember the animals which once roamed freely under their shelter?

### Page 5 - Photographer: Gary Smith

One of the first signs of spring, often as early as February, are the 'lamb's tail' catkins adorning hazel bushes, and the white flowers of blackthorn. Both are common hedgerow shrubs. When blackthorn flowers coincide with a spell of cold weather this is known as a blackthorn winter.

### Page 7 - Photographer: David North

Dawn and dusk, sunrise and sunset: magical times to be outdoors in the natural world and always the best times for encounters with wildlife.

### Page 9 - Photographer: Martin Hayward Smith

A fully open poppy flower keeps its petals for a single day only. Poppy seeds remain viable in the soil for decades, some perhaps even for as long as a century.

### Page 11 - Photographer: Chris Knights

As soon as a tractor ploughs a field, as if by some sixth sense, large numbers of gulls appear. They noisily follow the plough swooping down to seek earthworms and grubs in the newly-turned furrows.

### Page 12 - Photographer: Martin Hayward Smith

Only remnants still exist of once extensive heathlands. On a hot summer day birds fall silent in the middle of the day and these distinctive gorse and heather-clad open areas can appear devoid of life. In fact they are home to many special heathland creatures including nightjars, lizards and adders.

**Page 15 - Photographer: Brian Macfarlane.**

*Observing nature closely reveals new perspectives - reflections are like windows revealing new angles and hidden patterns.*

**Page 17 - Photographer: Chris Knights**

*In autumn and winter large flocks of crows - jackdaws, rooks and carrion crows - gather in fields at sunset, and then, as darkness falls, fly to communal woodland roosts.*

**Page 19 - Photographer: David North**

*Trees are the largest and longest living wild beings that most of us will meet. With effortless wisdom they perform the everyday miracles we rely on, providing us with oxygen, cleaning our air and giving us shade and shelter.*

**Page 20 - Photographer: Gary Smith**

*Snow buntings nest in the far north. Each winter small flocks arrive on the east coast of England and spend the winter feeding on seeds along the strandline. Holkham Bay in Norfolk is one of the best sites to spot this attractive black and white winter visitor.*

**Page 23 - Photographer: Simon Harrap**

*Bee orchid flowers mimic bumblebees. The resemblance of the flower to a bee, and the flower's scent which is similar to pheromones produced by female bees, deceives male bees into attempting to mate with the flower. In this way pollen is transferred from plant to plant.*

**Page 25 - Photographer: Emma Cooper**

*Blakeney Point was Norfolk's first nature reserve - acquired by the National Trust in 1912. It is a wild, romantic place of huge skies, strong winds and amazing sunsets. The line of shingle is home to nesting terns in summer and rare migrants in spring and autumn.*

**Page 27 - Photographer: Gary Smith**

In late April and early May bluebells transform woods with a haze of blue flowers. Britain has more bluebell woods than anywhere else in the world. They are one indicator plant of ancient undisturbed woodland, but are sensitive to trampling.

**Page 29 - Photographer: Tasha North**

Hedgerows can be very ancient landscape features, especially those along parish boundaries and ancient track-ways. Most hedgerows were originally planted of thorn but over centuries other tree and shrub species colonise naturally. A rule of thumb is that the number of species growing in a thirty metre section indicates the age of the hedge in centuries.

**Page 31 - Photographer: Gary Smith**

The red and white chalk cliffs at Hunstanton are the best place in Norfolk to watch nesting fulmars. These birds, once confined to remote Scottish islands, began breeding in Norfolk in 1965 and today several hundred can be found here.

**Page 32 - Photographers: (Clockwise from top left) David North, Chris Knights, Martin Hayward Smith, David North.**

In late winter ivy berries become a vital source of food for birds, especially wood pigeons and blackbirds. Wood pigeons cling on to the ivy with spread wings and gorge themselves on the berries.

**Page 35 - Photographer: Martin Hayward Smith**

In the evening and early morning pink-footed geese fly to and from traditional safe roost sites. More than a third of the world population winters along the North Norfolk coast and skeins of many thousands fill the sky - one of Britain's most inspiring winter wildlife spectacles.

**Page 37 - Photographer: Kevin Simmonds**

Most views of wild mammals are fleeting, yet these creatures, our nearest evolutionary relatives, are almost as widespread as birds. Their lives, often nocturnal, are mysterious to us, and usually only revealed through paw prints or at best a fleeting glimpse.

**Page 38 - Photographer: Chris Knights**

Male pheasants with their iridescent colours and bizarre red face wattles spend most of their time in Spring displaying to attract a harem of ten or a dozen drab brown females. They have no road sense and anyone who drives in rural Norfolk will be aware of just how many fall victim to passing cars.

**Page 39 - Photographer: Kevin Simmonds**

Noisy, screaming parties of swifts mark the arrival of summer. Swifts are the most aerial birds on the planet, sleeping, feeding and mating on the wing. Young swifts may fly for over a year without ever landing, crossing continents between Europe and Africa.

**Page 41 - Photographer: Martin Hayward Smith**

Swallowtails, Britain's largest butterfly, are now confined to the Norfolk Broads. Nature reserves such as Hickling and Ranworth Broads and Strumpshaw Fen are good places to look for this showy butterfly.

**Page 43 - Photographer: Brian Macfarlane**

Barn owls have the ability to fly soundlessly aided by soft, silky endings to their flight feathers which act as silencers on their wings. At rest their beautifully marked plumage can be fully appreciated but in flight they usually appear pure white.

Photo: Martin Hayward Smith

**Page 48 - Photographer: Martin Hayward Smith**

Reedbeds are rarely silent. Even the slightest breeze creates reed music from the swaying stems. In summer the living green reeds sigh softly. In winter the brittle, dry reeds play different tunes.

Photo: Kevin Simmonds

## Words on Wildlife

*Written* in Norfolk by **David North**
*Designed* in Norfolk by **Paul Westley**
*Printed* in Norfolk by **Crowes Complete Print**
*Inspired* by Norfolk's magical wildlife and wild places